Oh, Fudge!

A HIGH-CALORIE COMEDY

by Monk Ferris

SAMUEL FRENCH, INC.

45 West 25th Street — NEW YORK 10010

7623 Sunset Boulevard — HOLLYWOOD 90046

LONDON — *TORONTO*

Printed in U.S.A.
ISBN 0 573 69112 6

BILLING AND CREDIT REQUIREMENTS

All producers of OH FUDGE *must* give credit to the Author in all programs and in all instances in which the title of the Play appears for purposes of advertising, publicizing or otherwise exploiting the Play and/ or production. The author's name *must* appear on a separate line in which no other name appears, immediately following the title of the play, and *must* appear in size of type not less than fifty percent the size of title type.

"OH, FUDGE!"

Cast of Characters

DANNI DAWN, a lovely young star of TV commercials
CAMERON BARKLEY, her very friendly personal physician
HILARY CHARLES, an amiable superstar of the silver screen
BUGSY McCORKLE, Hilary's eager-beaver personal manager
AUGUSTA FAIRFAX, owner and proprietress of a Fat Farm
MABEL CHUBBS, a cheerful-but-plump registered nurse
ROMULUS BORK, a neanderthalic-behemoth attendant

LOCALE: The Fairfax Clinic for Digestive Psychoses (i.e.: a Fat Farm)
TIME: The Present

ACT ONE: Late afternoon in Danni's guest room at the clinic
ACT TWO: Early the following morning

Oh, Fudge!

ACT ONE

Curtain rises on a pleasant guest room at the "Fairfax Clinic for Digestive Psychoses" [*see Stage Setting*]*; all doors are closed and the drapes are drawn.* [*NOTE: If you want more lamps/lights in the room than indicated in the Stage Setting — such as a wall-mounted lamp over the writing desk — by all means include them; however, all these extra lamps must — just like the two bed-flanking lamps on the matched night tables — be controlled by the lightswitch beside the corridor door. Also, if a chest-of-drawers low enough so that its topside is on a level with the mattress — so there is no interference with sightlines to the bed — is hard to find, then either mount the bed upon a platform to bring it on a level with the chest,* or *simply use a bed-width bench in its place — we need a surface for luggage and/or sitting in this locale.*] *It is daylight outside the French doors, so the room is not completely dark; lighting will come up full when drapes open.*

At curtain-rise, room is untenanted. Then door L. *opens, and Nurse MABEL CHUBBS Enters; MABEL is 30–40 years old and as plump as her last name indicates* [*NOTE: This plumpness is* makeup*— cotton rolls in her cheeks, padded clothing, etc.*]*; she is in uniform — white dress and shoes, starched cap — so her career-choice is immediately evident. MABEL bustles over to* U.R.*, opens drapes, opens French doors wide* [*FULL LIGHTS*]*, steps to bed and unnecessarily pats/plumps exposed pillows,* *takes a backstep to observe her work, seems satisfied, then starts cross toward still-open door to corridor, but stops as AUGUSTA FAIRFAX steps into room. AUGUSTA is of late middle-age, tall and autocratic, and dressed anachronistically in a floor-length, long-sleeved, high collared gown; her hair is upswept and severe in style; her voice, however, is well-modulated and pleasant.*

AUGUSTA. All in readiness, Nurse Chubbs?

MABEL. Yes, Miss Fairfax.

AUGUSTA. Very well. (*turns toward corridor*) Come in, my dear.

(*A woman Enters, wearing a hat with a veil that hides her features, a long topcoat, and gloves; when this disguise is removed, this will prove to be DANNI DAWN, a lovely young lady in her mid-20s, with—if possible—a glorious cascade of blonde hair which will tumble free when hat is off.*)

DANNI. Oh, what a lovely room!

AUGUSTA. Of *course* it is, my dear. What were you expecting?

DANNI. Oh . . . *you* know—something like a monk's-cell—a bare cot and a high barred window. I've never been to a Fat Farm before. (*MABEL winces, and to a lesser degree so does AUGUSTA; then:*)

AUGUSTA. My dear—the Fairfax Clinic for Digestive Psychoses *may* assist in conquering a tendency toward avoirdupois, but we *never* use the term "Fat Farm" here.

MABEL. Not at *these* prices.

AUGUSTA. (*stung, but not unpleasant*) Mabel.

MABEL. Sorry.

AUGUSTA. I wonder what's keeping Romulus? (*peeks down corridor*) Ah, there he comes.

DANNI. "Romulus"?

MABEL. Romulus Bork. The man who took your luggage in the foyer.

DANNI. Do you know—when he *first* picked up my bag, I thought he was trying to *steal* it!

AUGUSTA. He *does* look dangerous, doesn't he! That's why I hired him. We sometimes need to keep certain of our guests—toeing the mark, if you follow me?

MABEL. When it comes to keeping people in line, a little terror goes a long way.

AUGUSTA. (*a little less pleasantly*) Mabel!

MABEL. (*with a slight cringe*) Sorry, Miss Fairfax.

(*Then ROMULUS BORK Enters; he gives the impression of being nine feet tall and four feet across the shoulders, like the captain of a neanderthal wrestling team; he wears an attendant's "dress whites" and totes a large suitcase as easily as if it were a helium balloon; DANNI and MABEL will do automatic backsteps from this presence, though AUGUSTA stands her ground, as he places suitcase on top of chest-of-drawers.*)

AUGUSTA. Thank you, Romulus.

ROMULUS. (*in a voice deep as a well*) No problem. (*turns, lumbers past AUGUSTA and out door* L.; *AUGUSTA will shut door behind him, as MABEL and DANNI both let out pent-up breaths*)

MABEL. Scary, isn't he!

DANNI. Very! (*will remove hat, then coat and gloves, all of which MABEL will take, over next few speeches*) Does he come around—*often* . . . ?

AUGUSTA. Not if you behave yourself.

DANNI. I'll behave.

MABEL. (*nods*) Everybody does. (*will take garments into closet*)

AUGUSTA. (*puzzled*) My dear—?

DANNI. (*fluffing out her hair with her fingers*) Yes—?

AUGUSTA. You—you *puzzle* me.

DANNI. I *puzzle* you? In what way?

AUGUSTA. Well, if you'll pardon my saying so, you don't seem to be a—um—*candidate* for a Fat Fa— That is, for a weight-control program such as we offer here.

MABEL. (*emerging from closet minus garments, and shutting door*) Matter of fact, you look downright *gorgeous*! (*takes closer look at her; then:*) And you look *extremely* familiar, too! But where could I have *seen* you?

DANNI. Does *this* help? (*takes grinning stance, facing us, with imaginary object held beside her face between thumb-and-fingers, as if for our observation*) "Yes! Dento-White sure helped *my* smile become the sexiest on the block!"

MABEL. Oh! Of course! You're that girl who sells everything from dog food to fork-lifts, always wearing a bikini!

AUGUSTA. So *that's* where I've seen your face—among other things—before! But, my dear, now I'm more baffled than ever! I mean, *you* have the kind of shape my *other* guests would *kill* to get! What in the *world* are you doing *here*?

DANNI. (*sighs, sits on chest beside suitcase*) I wish I knew! It's all a little frightening. But Doctor Barkley was so very *insistent* that I come that I was too afraid *not* to!

MABEL. Say, maybe it's anorexia nervosa! Do you feel

compelled to keep your weight down, avoid meals, starving yourself into dangerous malnutrition?

AUGUSTA. Really, Mabel, we mustn't make snap diagnoses about the young lady—oh, by the way, now that you're securely in your room with no more need for disguise—what is your *name,* dear?

DANNI. Danni Dawn. The trouble with commercials on TV is everybody gets to know your face, but hardly anybody knows your name. That's no way to get into the movies.

AUGUSTA. Ah! Becoming a movie star is your dream—?

MABEL. (*wistfully*) It's *everybody's* dream! (*then, brightening*) Why, do you know—*Hilary Charles* is staying with us! I'll bet *she* could give you some tips on how to get into pictures!

DANNI. Hilary Charles the movie star?! I had no *idea* she had a weight problem!

AUGUSTA. Nurse, you really *mustn't* discuss our guests!

MABEL. But Miss Fairfax, Danni will *meet* her at mealtime—*everyone* knows Hilary Charles on sight! And if she's staying *here,* well—

AUGUSTA. All right, all right, agreed! *All* our guests have weight problems. Except—(*frowns slightly at DANNI*) *you* certainly don't fit the category!

DANNI. Maybe Doctor Barkley will clear the mystery up—for *both* of us! Do you have any idea when he'll be arriving?

AUGUSTA. Let me see—when he first telephoned, it was about noon—and he was just about to leave and start up here. He was coming by car, I believe.

DANNI. Oh, good, then he should be here soon. (*stands*) I don't envy him the drive. I just spent five hours cooped up in the back of a limousine with drawn shades. It's not my idea of a fun-trip. And on top of everything, I'm absolutely *starving* to death! What time is dinner?

MABEL. Still almost an hour from now. But don't get your hopes up.

AUGUSTA. Really, Nurse Chubbs!

MABEL. Miss Fairfax, whatever the nutritional merits of our institution's output in the refectory, this *is* a place where people come to *lose weight* . . . !

DANNI. Oh, dear! You don't mean things like carrot-sticks and lettuce with no dressing?!

MABEL. I mean carrot-sticks *or* lettuce with no dressing!

DANNI. I *knew* I should've eaten lunch! (*sights phone, moves toward desk*) Maybe I can send out for pizza—!

AUGUSTA. (*not unkindly*) I'm afraid the delivery boy wouldn't get past the gates with it. Far too many of our guests tend to be —backsliders. There is absolutely *no* food admitted from outside.

DANNI. Isn't there even a candy-bar machine in the lobby?

MABEL. You've got to be kidding!

AUGUSTA. We never even *mention* the word "candy" at the clinic.

DANNI. (*slumps disconsolately into desk chair*) I don't suppose there's another limousine heading *back* to L.A.?

AUGUSTA. Not till tomorrow morning, I'm afraid. But I can hardly permit you to leave without Doctor Barkley's permission—

DANNI. You can't *keep* me here if I decide to go—can you?

AUGUSTA. Certainly *not.* But—if your doctor thinks you should *be* here—wouldn't it be better to wait until he arrives before you make that decision? I'm *only* thinking of your *health*—

DANNI. Then why won't you *feed* me?!

MABEL. Look, perhaps I can ask the kitchen staff to make you up a tray—

AUGUSTA. Mabel, dear, you *know* that's impossible! Until the doctor tells us Danni's dietary requirements—

MABEL. My dear, could you possibly tell us what your dietary problem *is*?

DANNI. (*stands, shakes her head helplessly*) Until this morning, I didn't even think I *had* a dietary problem!

MABEL. Then—why did you go to see Doctor Barkley in the *first* place?

DANNI. (*half-explaining, half-refreshing her own memory*) About a week ago, we were shooting this commercial in the Amazon jungle—for a *sneaker*-manufacturer. The idea was, I'd wear the company's sneakers and be able to out-run a charging alligator—

AUGUSTA. (*fascinated*) A *real* alligator?!

DANNI. That's the only kind they *have* in the Amazon!

MABEL. But isn't that rather—*dangerous*?

DANNI. Try telling that to the sponsor! If it sells the product, he's all for it! It's not as though *he* has to avoid those snapping jaws! Oh, of course, they had a crack shot with a rifle standing by, just in case—and the *money* was absolutely *fabulous*—

MABEL. If you lived to spend it!

DANNI. Listen, the *alligator* wasn't as dangerous as those *mosquitoes* down there! They're so big, they can't take off without filing a *flight*-plan! And I ran right into a whole *squadron* of them!

AUGUSTA. I *hope* you were wearing protective clothing—?

DANNI. You're joking. I'm Danni Dawn, remember? I have a certain—public image to uphold!

MABEL. You were wearing nothing but a *bikini*?!

DANNI. Well, I *did* have those *sneakers* on, of course.

AUGUSTA. Oh, you poor thing!

DANNI. (*sits glumly on chest*) Poorer than you know: I had so many lumps on my body that they had to *cancel* the shoot, and there went the paycheck! (*a little brighter*) But my time wasn't *totally* wasted—the director thinks they can use the footage for a *calomine* commercial—they'll show me smiling and lumpless, holding the bottle up for the world to admire—*if* I ever get *out* of this place! (*leans back so that her upper half now rests on the bed, wearily*)

AUGUSTA. I still don't see what that has to do with Doctor Barkley . . . ?

DANNI. (*still supine, talking toward the ceiling*) I picked up some kind of *bug*—from those mosquito-bites. Wasn't feeling exactly *rotten*, but very much not up to par, if you know what I mean. So I went to see the doctor, and he took some tests, and—well—the results came in this morning, and the next thing I knew I was in a coat, gloves, veil and limousine, headed *here*!

(*there is a KNOCK* [*actually, a heavy, hollow THUD-THUD-THUD*] *at door; DANNI sits up, a little startled, as AUGUSTA turns and goes to door*)

AUGUSTA. I wonder what *Romulus* wants—?

MABEL. Don't you wonder how she *knew* who's at the door?

DANNI. No. I've *seen* Romulus.

(*Then, as AUGUSTA opens door, DANNI stands up and*

joins MABEL in a kind of unified uneasy backstep from ROMULUS, who Enters carrying a large package in brown wrapping paper, which he will place on chest, during next few speeches.)

ROMULUS. Package came for Miss Dawn.

AUGUSTA. But Romulus—we *never* bring packages to guests without first inspecting their contents . . . ?!

ROMULUS. (*points at writing on package*) Said *not* to.

AUGUSTA. What?! Let me see that—(*leans over package and reads aloud:*) "Not to be opened by clinic staff, *especially* Miss Fairfax"! (*turns toward DANNI*) Now, really, my dear, did you think such a childish ploy would work?

DANNI. Me? Miss Fairfax, *I* don't know anything about this package!

MABEL. (*craning to see*) Does it say who sent it?

ROMULUS. (*points toward return-address area atop package*) Doctor Barkley.

MABEL. Well, then, it *must* be all right . . . ?

AUGUSTA. *If* it indeed *came* from Doctor Barkley. We'd better have a look.

ROMULUS. (*pointing at writing*) Said *not* to.

MABEL. Perhaps we *should* wait until the doctor arrives—

AUGUSTA. Nonsense. He wouldn't have any secrets from *us*! Open it, Romulus.

ROMULUS. Doctor be *mad* . . . ! (*but nevertheless, he takes hold of it, and somehow with a single two-handed tug has the wrappings torn completely free of the contents: six flat boxes which are easily recognizable as candy-boxes*)

MABEL. (*clasps hands to her breast with near-delirious joy*) It's *fudge*! (*as AUGUSTA gives her a look, unclasps hands and grows staid, for:*) Dear me, this will *never* do!

AUGUSTA. Danni, this is a *total* violation of our rules! Chocolate of *any* kind is *never* allowed on these premises!

DANNI. But honestly—I swear—I know *nothing* about this!

AUGUSTA. Nurse, take these things away at once! And be *careful*! (*as MABEL eagerly stacks boxes and starts for door, adds to DANNI:*) Some of our guests grow—*unruly* in the presence of chocolate . . .

MABEL. They'd *kill* for it! (*Exits through still-open door on:*) I hope I don't get mugged!

ROMULUS. (*still holding bunched-up halves of wrapping-paper*) What do with this?

AUGUSTA. Take it to my office and put it on the desk. I want to *show* it to Doctor Barkley when he arrives (*ROMULUS nods and Exits, leaving door still open*) Danni, you must understand that if we are to *help* you with your problem—

DANNI. (*very angry*) Read my lips: I . . . did . . . *not* . . . send . . . that . . . candy!

AUGUSTA. (*stares at her a second; then:*) Do you know—I *believe* you! But if you didn't—who *did? Who would*?

DANNI. (*somewhat mollified, shrugs*) Search *me*!

AUGUSTA. Oh, dear, that reminds me—we never *did* check the contents of your suitcase! (*steps to suitcase, touches locks, hesitates*) Do you mind?

DANNI. Of course not . . . though I'll bet you'd open it *anyway* even if I *did*!

AUGUSTA. Well . . . rules *are* rules. Just this week, one of our ladies actually packed a *pizza* in her suitcase!

DANNI. (*laughs*) It's all right. I understand. By all means, look!

AUGUSTA. Thank you.

(*Will proceed to open suitcase, rummaging through what turns out to be normal contents—clothing, toiletries, etc.—during:*)

DANNI. I *wonder* now . . . there are a lot of young ladies back in L.A. who'd *love* to take over where I left off . . . I mean, if I grew too *large* for that bikini, it'd be open season on all those commercials. My contract *does* have a *weight*-clause . . . !

AUGUSTA. (*completing inspection*) Ah! Then you think the fudge might have been sent by a *rival*—?

DANNI. It's the *likeliest* solution—except—

AUGUSTA. (*has finished inspection, straightens, but leaves suitcase open*) Except—?

DANNI. (*shrugs in bewilderment*) Who *knew* I was coming here today? Until a few hours ago, *I* didn't even know!

AUGUSTA. It *is* mysterious, isn't it!

DANNI. Perhaps Doctor Barkley *did* send it, after all!

AUGUSTA. Danni, *no* reputable physician would sent *fudge* to a *Fat Farm*—! I mean—to this clinic . . .

DANNI. Are you telling me you think Doctor Barkley is *dis*reputable—?

(*This is said, unfortunately, just as CAMERON BARKLEY—a medical man in his mid-30s, wearing a light topcoat and toting a medical bag—Enters* L.)

AUGUSTA. (*whose back is toward door, speaks even as DANNI sees entrant and reacts*) In all honesty, I must tell you that on occasion I've had some *nasty* surprises—!

CAMERON. (*pleasantly*) As nasty as *this*?

AUGUSTA. (*whirls to face him, staggers back a step*) Doctor Barkley!

CAMERON. (*will set medical bag atop desk, remove coat and drape it over desk chair, during:*) Yes, it's me, in the flesh—the *disreputable* flesh.

AUGUSTA. I really *must* apologize. We weren't actually *accusing*—just *theorizing*. I mean, when that package of *fudge* arrived—

CAMERON. Oh, good! I wasn't sure how fast that messenger service could get it here!

AUGUSTA. You mean—you *did* send it?!

CAMERON. Say—come to think of it—how did you *know* what was in the package? I distinctly marked it *not* to be opened by you or your staff! (*looks around*) And where *is* it, anyway!

AUGUSTA. Oh, dear! I had Nurse Chubbs take it away!

CAMERON. You let *Mabel* get her hands on thirty-seven dollars worth of *fudge*?! How long ago?

DANNI. You must have just *missed* her, Doctor—she went out just before you came in.

CAMERON. (*starts out door*) Then there's still time to catch her! Come *on*, Gus, help me look for her!

DANNI. (*as AUGUSTA starts following him out*) "Gus"?

AUGUSTA. (*manages a smile of chagrin*) Short for "Augusta," my given name. I *hate* people to call me that!

DANNI. "Augusta" or "Gus"?

AUGUSTA. What do *you* think!

CAMERON. (*off*) Gussie, what's *keeping* you—?!

AUGUSTA. Excuse me—! (*Exits, shutting door behind her*)

DANNI. (*musing, trying the sound on her tongue:*) "Gus Fairfax" . . . (*gives an amused chuckle*) Really takes the edge off all that austerity—! (*will now do some unpacking, taking toiletries kit, a robe and a pair of slip-*

pers into bathroom, opening door on:) Ah! This *is* the bathroom!

(*She will move from our view, and then HILARY CHARLES, an attractive woman in her early 30s, will appear at open French doors; she wears a sweat-suit and sneakers, and a look of sneaky desperation; after a quick look around, she rushes into room, peeks under bed, into closet, opens and closes a few drawers on the chest, and is just stooping to peek into the central desk-drawer when DANNI emerges from bathroom.*)

DANNI. (*studies her a second; then:*) Can I *help* you?

HILARY. (*straightens in shock, spins to face her*) *Oh*! I thought you'd gone *out*!

DANNI. (*reacting*) Hilary Charles!

HILARY. (*less upset by the recognition*) Are you impressed?

DANNI. Oh, Miss Charles—what an unexpected delight to meet you—in *person*! (*goes to her, takes her hands*) I've been a fan of yours for *years* and *years*—ever since I was a *little girl*—!

HILARY. (*not exactly pleased*) Please. I feel decrepit *enough* in this hell-hole, without being reminded of my *age*!

DANNI. But you *have* no age! You're young and beautiful and stunning as you were the first time I ever saw you in the movies! That was back in—

HILARY. Never *mind* when! . . . Please?

DANNI. (*laughs*) It doesn't matter. But truly—I can't get *over* how marvelous you look—have *always* looked—!

HILARY. (*with good humor*) You're doing it *again* . . .

DANNI. Oh, dear. I was *trying* to be *complimentary*—!

HILARY. And you *were*, darling, you *were*! It's just that I sort of hate to hear people mention the *length* of my lifelong career!

DANNI. But—if you'll pardon my asking—what were you *looking* for when I walked in?

DANNI. *Fudge*! I can sense the presence of chocolate fudge half a mile away! I can *smell* it! I thought you—as the new kid on the block—might have managed to smuggle some past old Gussie and her watchdogs! I'm *sure* I detected some—right in this room!

DANNI. Actually, you *did*—but Nurse Chubbs took it away.

HILARY. Oh, drat! (*starts toward French doors, her pace flagging and glum*) If *Mabel* took the fudge, we'll never see it again—*no one* will ever see it again!

DANNI. I'm *so* sorry!

HILARY. (*pauses midway between bed and closet*) Not *your* fault, kid. Say, what's your name, anyhow? You look oddly familiar.

DANNI. Danni Dawn. I do television commercials, Miss Charles.

HILARY. Oh, of course! Nice to meet you, Danni. And the name's Hilary.

DANNI. Hilary.

MABEL. (*off* U.R.) Well, how did *I* know it was doctor's orders—?!

HILARY. (*galvanized*) It's Mabel! I've got to get *out* of here! I'm supposed to be jogging around the gym!

DANNI. (*reaches for hall doorknob*) Hurry! This way!

HILARY. (*half-step that way, then full stop*) No! *Romulus* is on patrol! (*will duck into closet on:*) Excuse me,

Danni! I'll clear out soon as the coast is clear! (*shuts door after her, an instant before MABEL and AUGUSTA Enter* U.R. *through French doors, MABEL carrying five of the original six boxes*)

AUGUSTA. I only hope Doctor Barkley didn't *count* those boxes! How *could* you have eaten an *entire* box of fudge in such a short time?! (*sees DANNI, forces a weary smile*)

MABEL. You *told* me to get *rid* of the fudge. I *got* rid of the fudge. (*brief knocking at hall door*)

DANNI. *Come* in . . . ?

CAMERON. (*Enters room, shuts door behind him*) Ah! We weren't too late! I see you found the fudge intact!

AUGUSTA. Uh . . . *yes*! Here it is! Mabel—?

MABEL. (*crosses to CAMERON, hands boxes to him*) Here you are, Doctor. Sorry for the mixup.

CAMERON. That's all right, Mabel. You *thought* you were doing the right thing . . . That's odd, I thought I sent *six* boxes—?

DANNI. (*quickly*) Perhaps the supplier didn't *have* six boxes on hand!

CAMERON. Ah, yes, that must be it. Thank you, Mabel, that will be all. (*MABEL will Exit to hall, flashing a grateful smile at DANNI en route, closing door after her; CAMERON goes instantly conspiratorial*) Shut those doors and pull the drapes, Gussie! *No one* must know about this *fudge*! (*there is a muted groan from closet as AUGUSTA complies with his orders*) What was that?!

DANNI. (*quickly*) I'm *so* tired! That drive really took it out of me. Excuse me while I freshen up! (*starts into bathroom*)

AUGUSTA. Yes, of course, my dear! Why don't you have a nice relaxing shower!

DANNI. I believe I *will*! (*shuts bathroom door; CAMERON and AUGUSTA immediately converge below chest-of-drawers, and converse with lowered voices*)

CAMERON. That was quick thinking!

AUGUSTA. Well, from your attitude, I sensed you wanted a *private* conference.

CAMERON. Good girl! I have news—incredible news—downright fantastic news!

AUGUSTA. Just a moment—I can barely see your face! (*lights have dimmed, of course, when she closed drapes; she now hastens to lightswitch and turns room lighting up*) There, that's better! It'll be dark soon, anyway. (*returns to him below chest*) Now, Cameron, exactly *what* is going *on*!

CAMERON. Medical history! The results of Danni's tests were—well—*astounding*, this morning! (*flicks nervous glance toward bathroom, then continues*) I don't want her to know about those results just yet—it might interfere with my experiment, you understand.

AUGUSTA. No, I do *not* understand. What experiment, Cameron? What results?

CAMERON. (*gestures toward chest*) Sit down, Gussie, While I explain matters . . . (*she will sit obediently atop chest, but he will pace back and forth between desk and coffeetable, clasping and unclasping his hands, during:*) I suppose Danni told you about her short-lived jaunt up the Amazon?

AUGUSTA. About getting stung by those mosquitoes, you mean?

CAMERON. (*stops pacing near coffeetable*) Ah, good! Then I won't have to go over all *that* part of the story! (*sits on coffeetable, facing her*) Except it was *not* mosquitoes that stung her, Gussie. She's a bright girl, but hardly a qualified entomologist!

AUGUSTA. You mean an expert on bugs?

CAMERON. *Insects*. Bugs include things like spiders and scorpions and—

AUGUSTA. *Spare* me the lecture, please! I *know* the difference. I just wish you medical men would speak *plainly* about things.

CAMERON. Sorry. I guess I *do* grab for the four-dollar words when simpler words would do.

AUGUSTA. You certainly do! Now, please—what *was* Danni stung by, if not mosquitoes?

CAMERON. Are you familiar with a large yellow-orange insect with thin blue stripes known as—the *cocoa wasp*?

AUGUSTA. Not even slightly. But I'd certainly know one now if I encountered it. Sounds like a regular *rainbow*!

CAMERON. Oh, it *is*! That's how *I* knew what had stung Danni, the moment she described it!

AUGUSTA. *Come* now, Cameron, *you're* no entomologist, either!

CAMERON. Oh, all right—as soon as I looked it *up* in a book on bugs—

AUGUSTA. (*triumphantly*) *Aha*!

CAMERON. (*abashed*) I mean—*insects*! Satisfied?

AUGUSTA. Perfectly. But what has this yellow-orange-and-blue creature got to do with—?

CAMERON. (*comes to his feet, setting candy-boxes down at* U. *end of coffeetable*) *Everything*! I mean, in order to *treat* Danni, I had to know something about the *chemistry* of those stings—

AUGUSTA. The poor child! It must have been *dreadfully* painful!

CAMERON. Actually, no: The cocoa wasp's venom contains a kind of *anesthetic*, so the pain is minimal.

Which is *weird*, really, considering it seldom uses its sting except as an ovipositor!

AUGUSTA. As a what—?

CAMERON. Sorry. Four-dollar words again. It uses it for *egg*-laying, mostly.

AUGUSTA. Well, I should think its victim would *appreciate* being anesthetized, Cameron.

CAMERON. I doubt that very much, Gussie. The cocoa wasp only lays its eggs in cacao pods!

AUGUSTA. You mean those things that cocoa beans grow in?

CAMERON. Exactly! And surely the *pod* wouldn't feel anything, anesthetic or not!

AUGUSTA. Of course, we really know so *little* about the nervous systems of *plants*—

CAMERON. (*moves to chest, will sit beside her there, during:*) *That's* true enough, I daresay. But we're getting off the *point* of the story!

AUGUSTA. Which *is*—?

CAMERON. Have you ever seen photographs of the *natives* of the Amazon jungle, Gussie?

AUGUSTA. Are you changing the subject again?

(*Over next few speeches, we—but not they—will see closet door angle open slightly; then, after a moment, HILARY's arm will appear from behind* U. *end of settee, her hand will take top candy-box from stack, retreat with it, and closet door will slowly close again.*)

CAMERON. Not even slightly. I'm making a very important point!

AUGUSTA. Well, let me see, now—I can't remember the specific *tribes*, of course, but I *do* recall short little men dressed in next to nothing, with black oily hair, and woefully skinny arms and legs—

CAMERON. *Exactly*! Don't you see where this is all leading?

AUGUSTA. Frankly, no. What have those skinny little men got to do with cocoa wasps, or Danni, or—(*stops; thinks; her eyes widen; then:*) Cameron—are you suggesting that those *natives* are victims of the cocoa wasps—?

CAMERON. Those *skinny* natives!

AUGUSTA. Oh! Oh, dear! Do you mean that Danni—?

CAMERON. Is remaining *slender*—without gaining so much as an *ounce*—and yet, since her return, she's eaten almost *nothing but fudge*!

AUGUSTA. (*comes to her feet*) Cameron—are you telling me that the sting—or the chemicals from that sting—make it possible for a person to eat all the fudge they want and not gain weight?!

CAMERON. (*stands, takes her hands*) It's not that they *want* it, Gussie—they *must* have it! You wouldn't *believe* the test-results I saw this morning! Danni's bloodstream is swirling with some of the craziest chemicals I've ever encountered! Chemicals that thirst for caffeine, for theobromine, for heavy proteins and oils—

AUGUSTA. For *fudge*! So *that's* why you—(*has started gesturing toward stack on coffeetable, stops, peers a bit more closely, then steps over to coffeetable, on:*) Cameron, *how* many boxes did you say you ordered sent here?

CAMERON. Six. Why?

AUGUSTA. Because there are only *four* boxes here, now!

CAMERON. Impossible! (*hurries over, counts; then:*) I

don't understand—I could have *sworn* there were *five* in that stack—?!

AUGUSTA. Unless Mabel somehow contrived to take *another* one—! (*realizes, as he reacts and looks keenly at her*) Oops.

CAMERON. So there *were* six!

AUGUSTA. It was *my* fault. I didn't realize they'd come from *you*, so I told Nurse Chubbs to—

CAMERON. (*interrupts impatiently*) Yes-yes, I quite understand, as far as her devouring *one* boxful goes—but Mabel would *never* take *another* box once she knew I *had* ordered the fudge. Unless—?!

AUGUSTA. What *is* it, Cameron. Why do you look so uneasy? Unless *what*?

CAMERON. (*with the dawn of horror*) Unless she couldn't *help* herself! Oh, damn! (*smacks fist into palm*) What a shortsighted *fool* I've been! It never occurred to me till now that—

AUGUSTA. (*impatiently*) That *what*?!

CAMERON. (*faces her, announces solemnly:*) That Danni's condition might be . . . *contagious*!

AUGUSTA. (*reacts, a hand going to her mouth to semi-stifle a gasp; then:*) But—I thought you said—I mean, if those stings from the cocoa wasps were simply of a *chemical* nature, that is—

CAMERON. I know, I know! If it were only *chemistry* involved, another person couldn't catch the disease any more than they could catch *arsenic*-poisoning—! But if there are bacteria, or some new *virus* causing her condition—?!

AUGUSTA. Oh, this is monstrous! Exposing my guests to—to—(*stops the thought, thinks a moment; then:*) But you were so *sure* it was merely a *chemical* imbalance in her blood—?!

CAMERON. (*with self-scorn*) What did *I* know?! Gussie, this is a *brand-new* disease! A new frontier in internal medicine! How *could* I have been so smug to imagine I knew *anything* about it! I was so excited at the prospect —you know, getting written up in all the medical journals—maybe even having the condition *named* after me—"The Barkley Syndrome!"—for the discovery of a marvelous new blight upon the world's hygiene—

AUGUSTA. (*abruptly realizes, and interrupts:*) Cameron!

CAMERON. (*distracted*) What?

AUGUSTA. If it's *contagious*—why are we *standing* here?! We've got to catch *Mabel* before it spreads to every last guest in my *clinic*!

CAMERON. (*galvanized*) Good heavens, you're right! There's not a moment to lose! (*heads toward hall door*) I'll go this way, you go that way!

AUGUSTA. Right! I only pray we're not too late—!

(*He Exits to hall, closing door after him; she Exits to garden, first impatiently tugging drapes open* [*it is TWILIGHT OUTSIDE, now*] *then thrusting both French doors wide and vanishing through them off* R.*; a moment later, closet door opens and HILARY peers out cautiously, then tiptoes into room, clutching the stolen candy-box to her chest; she looks around for a place to put it—or dispose of it—then finally shrugs and sets it atop the four other boxes; at this juncture, DANNI—now in her bathrobe and slippers—emerges from bathroom, sees HILARY, and:*)

DANNI. Oh, good, they've gone! I was so afraid they'd catch you!

HILARY. I was lucky. Oh—I should apologize—

(*gestures toward stack*) I had some of your fudge. Only four pieces. (*hugs herself swooningly*) It was *heavenly*!

DANNI. Don't apologize. Have it *all* if you want. I can't *stand* the stuff!

HILARY. *What*? But—from what Barkley and Gussie were saying—I thought you had an almost uncontrollable *craving* for fudge—like any normal decent woman.

DANNI. They both said *that*?!

HILARY. Well, *he* did. He said you absolutely *had* to have it, so I assumed—

DANNI. He meant that as a *medical* necessity. I mean, I'm *supposed* to have it—*he* says.

HILARY. Then why aren't you dancing in the streets? To be *commanded* to eat fudge—that's what every woman *dreams* of!

DANNI. (*sits on chest, glumly*) You'd think so, wouldn't you! But—I guess—that's the whole *problem*! It's weird, I know, but when you absolutely *have* to eat something—especially on doctor's orders—you can't *stand* it!

HILARY. (*sits beside her, amazed*) *Fudge*—?!

DANNI. (*nods sadly*) Even fudge. It's like—well—fudge has always been a *sneaky* kind of pleasure. I mean, every time I'd succumb, over all my own good counsel, to *have* a piece of it—fully knowing it meant an extra half hour's jogging or situps to compensate for it—it was a kind of delicious *delight*! But to mechanically just sit and have piece after piece—I don't know—it takes all the *fun* out of it, somehow.

HILARY. (*inspired*) The old Forbidden Fruit problem!

DANNI. Yes! That's it! That's *exactly* it! The more I knew I shouldn't—the more I wanted to! But now—now that I *have* to sit and eat the stuff—I get almost sick to my stomach when mealtime approaches. Stupid, isn't it!

HILARY. (*thoughtfully*) No, It makes sense. It's like autographs.

DANNI. Autographs?

HILARY. When I was still a struggling unknown bit-player, I used to *long* for the day I'd be famous, a household word, recognizable on sight whenever I went out, people just clamoring for my autograph . . . Well—I *got* my wish—and now I want to run and *hide* when I see a mob of fans descending upon me with their autograph books at the ready!

DANNI. I guess it's human nature, Hilary. The less we have of something, the more we want it—but the more we have of it—oh, except maybe something like *money*—!

HILARY. Amen!

DANNI. —the less appeal it has for us anymore!

HILARY. (*pats DANNI on the knee, stands*) Life really stinks, doesn't it! Here *I* am, afraid of gaining even an *ounce* too much, hardly daring to *look* at the stuff, and there *you* are, getting *nauseous* at the prospect of having some, and your figure is absolutely *gorgeous*! (*looks at her, puzzled*) Say, that *is* odd, come to think of it. I mean, why *aren't* you ballooning like an inflatable liferaft?

DANNI. (*frowns out front*) I have no idea! I never thought about that part of it till you mentioned it. I *should* be approaching the *half-ton* mark by now—if calorie-counting means anything! (*stands*) See, when I *went* to the doctor, feeling kind of under par, about a week ago, I was *already* on a binge—kept eating fudge like crazy—and of course, when I told him about it, he very medically and solemnly told me to stop doing it at once! Being human, of course, I *didn't* stop—I must've gone through seven *pounds* of it before this morning, when I went back for my test-results—and then, without warning, he *told* me to have some—said I should go out, buy a pound of the stuff, eat it all, then get the hell out to *this* place by the next limousine! Doctors! Go figure 'em!

HILARY. But Danni—what did you *expect* him to say, under the circumstances—Oh! (*puts a hand to her mouth*) I forgot! You don't *know* what your problem is!

DANNI. And *you do*? What is it, tell me!

HILARY. Oh, kid—I can't! From what I overheard in that closet—Barkley doesn't *want* you to know—not yet, at least. And I'd hate to mess up your situation even more. I mean, if the doctor knows what he's doing, it's better for you to be kept in the dark about it.

DANNI. Oh, *please*, Hilary! Can't you even give me some kind of *hint*?

HILARY. Well—(*debates with herself; then:*) At *least* we know it's not contagious . . . darn it all. I would *love* to catch it!

DANNI. *How* do we know?

HILARY. They only *think* it is, because they don't know *I* filched the fudge while they were talking. See, they think Chubbs took it because she's got an uncontrollable *urge* for the stuff now, inherited from her contact with *you*, do you see? They're out scouting for her right this minute.

DANNI. Poor Mabel. I hope they *believe* her when she denies it! But *can't* you tell me—

HILARY. No. I'd better not. I may have gabbed too much already! (*starts backing toward* U.R.) Listen, Danni, I have to go get out of these sweats for dinner—you'd better get dressed yourself—if you want to talk some more, afterwards, we can stroll around the grounds. Maybe by then Barkley will have leveled with you.

DANNI. But Hilary—it's *my* problem—don't *I* have more right to know than *anybody*?

HILARY. I'm not sure. And I don't want to make a mistake, where your health is concerned.

DANNI. (*reluctantly*) All right. But let's make it a *long* talk!

HILARY. Actually, we'll only have about half an hour. After that, all the guests are locked in their rooms for the night.

DANNI. Locked in?! Why?

HILARY. There's a town within walking distance of the grounds. It has a soda fountain and a pizzeria.

DANNI. Even so — to be locked in —! What if there's a fire?

HILARY. Oh, it's not so dangerous as all that. See, only these garden doors get locked — some kind of automatic electronic system does it — but it's keyed to the fire alarm, so if there *is* any danger, all the locks open by themselves. I hope.

DANNI. But if the *hall* doors aren't locked, what's to prevent people from —

HILARY. *Romulus* is on patrol. All night.

DANNI. (*shivers*) They think of everything, don't they!

HILARY. Darn near. (*starts* U.R. *again*) But don't worry. We've got a full half-hour after dinner before lockup-time. If Barkley hasn't told you by then — maybe *I* will.

(*HILARY halts abruptly as BUGSY McCORKLE starts crossing by the open doors, spots her, checks his progress and instead Enters room; BUGSY is 40ish, in all non-matching garb-elements — brown sandals, yellow socks, purple pants, red-and-white-checked sports jacket, hot pink shirt, and very large sunglasses despite the exterior twilight; if he looks *like a Hollywood promoter-type, it's because that's what he is.*)

BUGSY. Hilary-baby!

HILARY. Bugsy! What are *you* doing here?!

BUGSY. Had to talk, quick. Your agent just landed you a fantastic deal with Paramount; the bucks are good, but I'm holding out for a percentage of the take, besides. Had to have your okay, though, before I started turning the screws—(*spots DANNI*) Oh, Hello.

HILARY. Danni Dawn—Bugsy McCorkle, my manager.

DANNI. How do you do—?

HILARY. Listen, we can't talk here, I've got to change for dinner. Come on over to *my* room and we'll hash this out. (*waves to DANNI as they Exit* U.R.) See you later, kid!

BUGSY. (*as they vanish off* R.)I just wasted twenty minutes running around the gym looking for you! What the heck were you doing in *her* room, sweetheart? (*They are gone; DANNI moves to suitcase, and is just selecting a dress to wear to dinner when there comes a KNOCK on the hall door.*)

DANNI. Come in . . . ?

MABEL. (*Enters, shutting door behind her*) Just wanted to let you know that it's dinner-time, dear. Shall I wait and show you the way to the refectory?

DANNI. Yes, thank you, nurse, that would be kind of you—*oh*—did you know Doctor Barkley and Miss Fairfax are both out *looking* for you?

MABEL. *Now* what'd I do?!

DANNI. It's all a mistake, really, something about a missing box of fudge.

MABEL. But I *told* them about that!

DANNI. There was *another* one missing—(*sees*

MABEL look toward stack)—but it was all a mistake. I think, though, that you should find them and clear matters up.

MABEL. (*starts for bathroom*) Soon as I have a drink of water. The first box made me so *thirsty*, but I haven't had a chance to—(*pauses*) That is, if you don't mind?

DANNI. Be my guest. I hope you don't mind *sharing*, though. I just brushed my teeth and rinsed.

MABEL. (*laughs*) If nurses worried about germs the way they *ought* to, there wouldn't *be* any nurses! (*Exits into bathroom, on:*) Thanks. (*an instant later, BUGSY, alone, dashes in* U.R.)

BUGSY. Miss Dawn! We've got to *talk*! Hilary just told me about your—(*notices she's making frantic signals to him re the bathroom, and then recoils as he hears:*)

MABEL. (*off*) Who's *that* you're talking to?

BUGSY. Yipe! Excuse me! (*ducks into closet, shuts door, simultaneous with:*)

DANNI. (*belatedly*) But—?! (*then she spins to face MABEL just emerging from bathroom*) Talking to? *I* wasn't talking to *anybody*, nurse.

MABEL. I could have sworn—?! Of course, it's hard to be sure with the water running. Well, now, you hurry and get ready for dinner, and I'll be right back to take you there, just as soon as I find Miss Fairfax or your doctor and clear things up! (*Exits to hall*)

DANNI. (*moves to closet, opens door on:*) Mister McCorkle, we can't *possibly* talk now! I've got to change my clothes, and—(*there is a knock at hall door; we barely see BUGSY just starting to emerge before DANNI shuts him into closet again, on:*) Jiggers! Another caller! . . . Just a *minute* . . . ! (*DANNI goes to door, opens it, and CAMERON—toting a napkin-covered tray of food—steps in*)

CAMERON. I thought I'd join you for dinner. (*will*

move to desk and set tray there as she closes door again, during:)

DANNI. But *I* was just getting changed to *go* to dinner!

CAMERON. What? *Go* to dinner? Oh, no-no-no, that's quite impossible. Not until we're certain your condition isn't contagious.

DANNI. Damn. (*then, curious*) What did you *bring* me, anyhow?

CAMERON. Bring you? Oh, you mean the *tray*! That's not for you. That's *my* dinner!

DANNI. So where's *mine*?!

CAMERON. (*indicates stack*) Right over *there*, of course.

DANNI. *Fudge*?! Doctor, I can't even *look* at another piece of fudge!

CAMERON. I'm afraid you have no choice, Danni. Under the circumstances—(*reacts belatedly to stack*) Where did that *fifth* box come from? I could have sworn—

DANNI. It's all been a mistake. Nurse Chubbs *didn't* take another box, after all.

CAMERON. Wow, is *she* going to be upset! I just met her in the hall and had her go for a *blood*-test! I was afraid she might have *caught* something from you, and—

DANNI. But she *knows* she didn't eat any fudge besides that *first* box. Why would she *go*?

CAMERON. (*guiltily*) I had—uh—I had *Romulus* take her to the lab. Never heard a nurse *scream* before.

DANNI. The poor thing. Still, I rather thought nurses took things like blood-tests as a matter of course.

CAMERON. Not when they're on the *front* end of the needle!

DANNI. (*plunks herself down disconsolately on chest*) I

never in my life thought I'd be unhappy because I *had* to eat fudge—!

CAMERON. (*reacts*) *Who told* you that?!

DANNI. Why—*you* did, Doctor!

CAMERON. *I* did—? *Oh*! You mean "had to" as doctor's orders! *I* thought you meant—uh—

DANNI. Yes? What exactly *did* you think I meant, Doctor? What's *wrong* with me, anyhow?

CAMERON. I—I didn't really want to *tell* you—afraid it might affect the tests and all—but on the other hand, if you're *upset* about the situation, *that* could adversely affect your endocrine system, too—

DANNI. (*stands*) Sometimes you doctors drive people *loony*, do you know that?! You're really no better than the old *witch*-doctors in primitive tribes, always sacrificing the loveliest maiden to the *volcano* whenever things go wrong!

CAMERON. Volcano? What are you talking about?

DANNI. Well, when was the last time a doctor told a patient he had to give up things like *parsnips*—or *tofu*—or *Brussells sprouts*?

CAMERON. Danni, you're not making sense!

DANNI. Of *course* I am! You always start having the person sacrifice the *nice* things—like *coffee* or *smoking*—or *red meat* or *liquor*—! Far as I'm concerned, you haven't progressed very far from maidens-into-the-volcano!

CAMERON. Now, wait—it's not the same thing at all—science has come a long way since the time when—

DANNI. Don't hand me that! If science is so smart, why doesn't a doctor ever prescribe medicine that will *cure* you for *sure*?

CAMERON. But—we *do* . . . don't we?

DANNI. You do *not*! You write out the prescription and say—"Here, *try this*, and we'll see what happens"!

CAMERON. (*abashed*) We *do* talk like that, don't we!

DANNI. Maybe that's why you're called a *practicing* physician! You're practicing on *me*!

CAMERON. (*turns, picks up tray from desk*) Maybe I'd better come back later, when you've calmed down a bit.

DANNI. Fine! but don't expect me to have any more *fudge*!

CAMERON. Now-now, that's just the "veggie syndrome" talking!

DANNI. The *what*?

CAMERON. Little children are naturally curious, want to try *everything*—but when a parent *insists* they eat their veggies, they immediately *refuse*. I remember a cartoon I once saw—a little girl is shoving her plate away and saying, "I don't *want* to grow up to be big and strong—I want to be pale and interesting!"

DANNI. (*laughs, despite her mood; then:*) I know *exactly* how that little girl felt!

CAMERON. Then please—*eat* your fudge. Actually, except for the calorie-count, it's really *very good* for your mood—chocolate is full of phenylethylamine [pr: feen-'l-ETH-'l-uh-meen], a known mood-altering drug. It affects the brain's pleasure-centers, makes you feel optimistic, sociable, peppy—

DANNI. (*dryly*) You mean like Nurse Chubbs on her way to that blood-test? And *she* just had an entire *box* of the stuff!

CAMERON. Her adrenalin kicked in. Terror has a way of doing that to people. (*is balancing tray on one hand, opening hall door with the other*) It's a powerful stimulant to help people get enough sudden energy to flee for their lives in an emergency.

DANNI. I sure wish you'd prescribe me some of *that*!

CAMERON. Now-now—eat the nice fudge—I'll be back later on, and then we'll talk.

DANNI. Damn *right* we will! *I* want to know what's going *on* with me!

CAMERON. Fair enough. I think I'd *better* tell you. But first—the *fudge*! (*nods toward stack, then Exits to hall, closing door after him*)

DANNI. (*stands irresolute; then turns and looks toward stack; then shrugs and heads toward it, on:*) Hell, I might as well. It beats *starving* to death! (*then she jumps back as BUGSY pops out of closet*) *Oh*! . . . Oh, sorry, Mister McCorkle, I forgot you were *in* there!

BUGSY. Sure-sure, that's okay, kid. Listen, I've got to talk to you, fast, before Barkley gets back here!

DANNI. What *is* it about me?! Everybody wants to *talk* to me!

HILARY. (*appears at French doors, now dressed spectacularly for dinner, hurries into room on her line:*) *Bugsy*, you've got to get *out* of here! Visiting hours are over the moment *dinner* is due!

BUGSY. Are you kidding?! *This* is the chance of a *lifetime*! The *hell* with the rules!

DANNI. What are you *talking* about?

BUGSY. See, it's this way, kid—if I understand your condition correctly—

HILARY. (*tugs at his arm*) Bugsy, not *now*! Write her a *letter*! Gussie doesn't *like* guests who disrupt the routine, and I *need* to get this extra poundage off me!

DANNI. You're joking! Your figure is *astonishingly* good!

HILARY. Maybe in *person*, honey, but not on the silver screen! The camera adds *ten pounds* to a performer—

except in 3-D movies, but how often do *they* get made these days?!

BUGSY. Hilary, in the time we've wasted *arguing*, I could have *said* my piece!

HILARY. Oh, all right, all right—but *hurry*! (*will step back to peer nervously out into garden, during:*)

BUGSY. It's like this, Miss Dawn—I'm a promoter—a guy with an eye on big bucks—and—

HILARY. (*reacts, dashes into room*) *Gussie's* coming down the path! Into the closet, quick! (*shoves BUGSY toward closet, starts following him in, stops for:*)

DANNI. Hilary, why are *you* hiding?

HILARY. If Gussie sees me anywhere near that *fudge*, she'll boot me right out of the clinic! (*abruptly smiles*) So—what've I got to *lose*?! (*grabs top box from stack, vanishes into closet with it, shuts door; an instant later, AUGUSTA appears in garden, Enters room*)

AUGUSTA. Not dressed, Danni? I was going to escort you to dinner.

DANNI. I don't *get* any dinner.

AUGUSTA. (*has turned and is closing French doors, now*) You don't? What makes you say *that*?

DANNI. Doctor Barkley. He insists I have nothing but *fudge*!

AUGUSTA. (*will now draw drapes across closed doors*) Well, I *guess* he knows what he's doing . . .

DANNI. I wish I *knew* he knows what he's doing!

AUGUSTA. (*starts across room toward hall door*) Don't fret, my dear. There are other guests in my clinic who would *die* to have a piece of fudge! Consider yourself lucky!

DANNI. But I'm so *sick* of the stuff—!

AUGUSTA. Nevertheless, if that's what the doctor

ordered— Oh, did anyone explain to you about the garden doors—?

DANNI. Uh—*yes*! You mean about them being locked after dinner, right?

AUGUSTA. That's right, dear. I just didn't want you to worry when they didn't open. Enjoy your fudge! (*Exits to hall; the instant the door closes, HILARY and BUGSY emerge from closet; HILARY has a happy smile, and replaces box atop stack.*)

BUGSY. Now, listen, I'll say this quick as possible—!

(*Hall door starts to open; HILARY and BUGSY gasp, turn tail and rush back into closet, shutting the door just as AUGUSTA pops in from hall.*)

AUGUSTA. I forgot to ask you—have you seen Nurse Chubbs anyplace?

DANNI. Doctor Barkley—sent her to the lab for a blood-test.

AUGUSTA. Ah! Do you know—I *thought* those screams were familiar! Well, happy fudge! (*Exits to hall again, shuts door; HILARY and BUGSY re-emerge.*)

HILARY. *I* don't get this much exercise *jogging*!

DANNI. Maybe it's a whole new approach to weight-reduction—the *closet-and-fudge* exercise!

HILARY. Wouldn't that be *wonderful*?!

BUGSY. I thought you were in a hurry?

HILARY. Sorry. Quick, speak your piece, then get *out* of here!

DANNI. Yes, just what *is* it you're trying to tell me?

BUGSY. Well, as a promoter, it seems to me that your problem is something downright *terrific*—something brand-new—unheard-of before—something that will really make *headlines* when the news comes out—

HILARY. Get to the *point*, Bugsy!

BUGSY. Okay-okay! Miss Dawn, it's *this* way—(*a knock at hall door*)

HILARY. Now, why did I just *know* that was going to happen?! (*but already has BUGSY's hand, and the box of fudge from the top of the stack in the other, and will lead him into closet and shut door, during:*)

DANNI. (*leaning close to hall door, her voice a [feigned] careless lilt:*) Who *is* it . . . ?

CAMERON. (*off*) Doctor Barkley! Are you decent?

DANNI. That never stopped you *before*! (*opens door*) Come in, come in! (*CAMERON Enters, carrying some bright, folded garments in his hands.*) What are those?

CAMERON. Pajamas.

DANNI. I already *have* pajamas, thank you.

CAMERON. (*as she shuts door again*) They're not for you.

DANNI. Then for who?

CAMERON. For *me*. I should have explained—I'm staying *here* tonight.

DANNI. Now *just* a *min*-ute—!

CAMERON. I assure you I have *no* designs on you!

DANNI. What's your plan? We toast marshmallows and sing camp-songs?

CAMERON. I have to keep you under *observation*. And, considering your condition may well be *contagious*, I cannot allow anyone *else* to keep coming in and out of here, until I know for sure!

DANNI. Damn it all—*what* condition?! Or do you plan to carry the secret to your *grave*—where I may very well *put* you if you don't *level* with me!

CAMERON. (*after a fractional hesitation*) All right.

(*Over his speech, he will take his topcoat from chairback, fold it, and place it atop desk beside his medical bag, and the pajamas beside them.*) Those weren't mosquitoes you ran into. They were cocoa wasps. The cocoa wasp lays its eggs in the cacao pod, and the larvae develop there. As they grow, they have *only* the cacao bean to live on. Somehow, after they pupate and emerge from the pod, their lymphatic systems *invert* this chemistry, producing a venom that *requires* the constituents of the cacao bean to neutralize its poison. That's what got into you. And that's why you *must* have chocolate to survive! (*turns to face her*) Any questions?

DANNI. (*who has been watching his movements with distrust*) Yes. Just *where* do you propose to *sleep*?

CAMERON. Haven't you heard *anything* I just said?!

DANNI. Every word of it. This is more important!

CAMERON. Now, really, Miss Dawn—

DANNI. Isn't that a rather *formal* way to address your *roommate*?

CAMERON. Danni. I assure you, I am doing this for *science*!

DANNI. That's fine for *you*. But why am *I* doing it?

CAMERON. Because you're a sensible young lady who wants to get *well, that's* why!

DANNI. Can't you observe me in the *morning*?

CAMERON. It's safer if I'm right here, in case you experience a medical *emergency*!

DANNI. Like fighting off your advances?

CAMERON. What makes you think I'd make advances?

DANNI. Do you *always* keep a pair of pajamas at the clinic?!

CAMERON. I borrowed those from Romulus!

DANNI. Romulus?! We could *both* get into them! (*half*

a second later:) Strike that. (*at that moment, loud bell rings for a few seconds; then*) What was that?

CAMERON. Lockup time. The garden doors are all sealed now.

DANNI. (*with a glance toward the closet, then quickly away from it*) But—they *can't* be! I mean—I get claustrophobia! Isn't there some way to leave mine unlocked?

CAMERON. Not without rewiring the clinic's entire electrical system. Now, just relax, get into bed, and I'll tell you a few things you should know.

DANNI. The only thing I want to know is where you intend to *sleep*!

CAMERON. On that *sofa*, of course!

DANNI. *That* little thing? You wouldn't be able to fit Romulus's *pajamas* onto that!

CAMERON. (*stiffly*) I . . . will . . . *manage*! All right?

DANNI. . . . All right. Now, what things did you want to tell me?

CAMERON. I'm worried about possible *contagion*. It's not as if you had a virus or anything that could be contracted by others in the usual sense—but a chemical imbalance is sure to show up in things like your perspiration, your saliva, the normal skin oil from the sebaceous glands—things like that. If you handle *food*, for instance, any person eating that food would get your chemistry into their system. If a person had a scratch, and you happened to cry, and your tears got into that scratch—or if you *kissed* somebody—or—

DANNI. I get it, I get it! I'm a walking *fudge*-bomb!

CAMERON. So far, we've been lucky. But I must insist on *total* isolation for you until I can learn *more* about your condition—how to prevent its spreading to *others*—

DANNI. Aren't *you* afraid of catching it?

CAMERON. Of course I am. But *someone's* got to check you out! It may as well be me.

DANNI. (*brightens*) Well! I guess I was *unduly* worried about your *advances*! One red-hot kiss, and it's fudge-time for *two*!

CAMERON. Exactly! Now, you'd better get some rest. We have a regular battery of tests I'm going to make in the morning.

DANNI. Whatever you say, Doctor. (*pulls down blanket, slips out of slippers, slides under blanket in her robe, pulls it up near her chin*) You know—as *silly* as this situation is—it's really rather *courageous* of you . . .

CAMERON. (*pleased, tries not to show it*) It's—nothing. Now, would you please turn over, or shut your eyes or something, while I get undressed?

DANNI. (*sits up, starting to enjoy the setup*) Why? *You* never shut your eyes when *I* undress!

CAMERON. *That* is a *doctor-patient* relationship!

DANNI. (*shrugs*) So is *this*!

CAMERON. It's *not* the same!

DANNI. But when *I've* undressed at your office in town, you always tell me the human body is nothing to be *ashamed* of!

CAMERON. I was talking about *your* body! Now, will you turn around or not?!

DANNI. Why, Doctor! You mean you *like* my figure?

CAMERON. It's sensational! *Satisfied*?! (*abruptly grabs up topcoat from desk*) This is going to wrinkle.

DANNI. Do you mean it's sensationally *healthy*, or do you mean—

CAMERON. You know damn well what I mean! I may be a doctor, but I'm also a man! (*starts across room, unfolding topcoat as he goes*) I'd better hang this up!

DANNI. (*realizes,* leaps *out of bed and beats him to the closet door, on:*) *No*! Let *me* do it! (*grabs topcoat out of his hands*) After all, you're a *guest* in my room!

CAMERON. (*startled, but pleased*) Then you don't *mind* my staying here tonight?

DANNI. (*with slight mockery of his earlier tone:*) I may be a patient—but I'm also a woman!

CAMERON. Aw, hell, you're making fun of me! (*turns away; at that instant, closet door opens and HILARY grabs coat from DANNI, pops back into closet and shuts door; he hears door, turns*) Boy, *that* was fast! What did you *do*, just *throw* it inside?

DANNI. It's all nicely hung on a *hanger*, and even buttoned up!

CAMERON. Impossible! Let me see—! (*starts for closet door, DANNI grabs him, spins him around so his back is to closet, flings her arms around him amorously*)

DANNI. Don't you *trust* me? (*behind him, HILARY pops out with hangered topcoat, thrusts it into DANNI's hands, pops—more quietly this time—back into closet*)

CAMERON. Danni—you're so soft—so warm—so near—!

DANNI. (*pulls back out of embrace, on:*) Don't forget "so *efficient*"! (*holds up topcoat for his gape-jawed perusal*)

CAMERON. How did you *do* that?!

DANNI. Professional models are *very* limber!

CAMERON. Do it again! I want to see! Please?

DANNI. (*avoiding closet-intrigue, heads for desk with coat*) *This* material won't wrinkle. Let's leave it where it was! (*drapes it, hanger and all, over chairback, then hops back into bed again*)

CAMERON. Well! I guess we're right back where we *started*! Now, are you going to demurely look the other way while I undress, or aren't you?!

DANNI. (*draws up her knees to her chest, hugs them with her arms, grinning*) I haven't quite decided . . . !

CAMERON. (*angrily moves toward desk*) All right, then, I'll change in the bathroom! (*grabs pajamas, starts for bathroom*)

DANNI. Party-pooper! (*CAMERON pauses to scowl at her, then Exits into bathroom and slams door; instantly, DANNI flips back blanket and jumps off* R. *side of bed, even as HILARY and BUGSY surge out of closet.*) You've got to get *out* of here!

HILARY. *How*? The garden doors are locked and Romulus is patrolling the halls!

BUGSY. *Forget* all that! We've got to *talk*! (*grabs DANNI's hands firmly but gently*) Then I want *you* to get out of here *with* us!

DANNI. *Me*? What for?

BUGSY. How thick-headed *are* you?! That man in there is trying to *cure* you! *This* man wants to make you the richest woman on the face of the earth! *Please* say I can be your manager!

DANNI. Mister McCorkle, what are you so *excited* about?

BUGSY. Haven't you realized your potential *yet*?! Right now, you could get five thousand dollars an hour from *any* candy manufacturer in the country, just for standing on the assembly line and *handling* the chocolates as they slide by!

DANNI. *What*?!

BUGSY. Don't you *get* it?! If you touch the candy, anyone who eats it becomes an *addict*! They'll *have* to have chocolate! The candy people will make more money than IBM!

HILARY. But Bugsy—if she starts an *epidemic* of chocolate-addiction—what about people who don't normally have easy *access* to chocolate?!

BUGSY. Like who?

HILARY. Oh—*desert* tribes—*eskimos*—! How are *they* going to fulfill their craving?

BUGSY. (*agitated by her attitude*) They'll *manage*! Okay?! (*back to DANNI*) You've *got* to do this, Danni! The world's been *waiting* for a good excuse to eat all the chocolate they want! They'll build a *monument* to you!

DANNI. Wait—you're talking too fast—let me think—!

BUGSY. What's to *think* about?! Kiddo, you're going to be *rich*! Hell, you could peddle your *saliva* for ten thousand dollars a *spit*!

DANNI. This is crazy! I mean, we're not even *sure* that I'm *contagious*! It's *only* a *theory*!

BUGSY. That's what they used to say about *space* travel! Danni, this thing is a *bonanza*!

DANNI. But what about calories—overweight—heart disease—?!

HILARY. (*beginning to catch BUGSY's enthusiasm*) No problem! I *heard* what Gussie said when I was in the closet—people can eat all the fudge they want and *not gain weight*!

BUGSY. Look, first let's concentrate on getting *out* of here, and *then* we'll iron out the nitty-gritty details.

DANNI. But unless we're absolutely *sure*—? (*then there is a THUD-THUD-THUD at hall door*)

TRIO. *Romulus*!

(*Door starts to open; there's no time for the closet: HILARY and BUGSY dive to the floor and huddle against R. side of bed, while DANNI steps quickly to area just below chest as a rather frantic ROMULUS lurches into the room.*)

ROMULUS. *Where* Doctor Barkley?!

DANNI. (*points*) In the *bathroom*!

ROMULUS. Must see him! (*starts for bathroom*)

DANNI. Romulus, is there anything *wrong*?

ROMULUS. (*pauses at bathroom door*) *Plenty* wrong! (*points toward still-open hall door*) Big problem with *Mabel*! (*then he opens bathroom door and steps inside*)

CAMERON. (*off*) *Heyyyy*! You could have *knocked*!

ROMULUS. (*still in our view, looking off* L. *into bathroom*) No time! Big problem! Mabel!

CAMERON. (*off*) *What* problem?!

ROMULUS. Come see!

(*By now, a curious HILARY and BUGSY have raised up on hands and knees to peek toward bathroom across bed; and then MABEL Enters from hall, weeping piteously; and* what *a MABEL!: Under her nurse's cap, her hair—previously culred tightly against her head—is now hanging long and luxurious, her face is slim and pretty, and her figure—we can tell even under the belt-tightened oversized-for-her-now uniform—is svelte and gorgeous.*)

DANNI/HILARY/BUGSY. *Ma-bel*—?!

MABEL. (*sobbing*) What am I going to *do*?! Whatever am I going to *do*?!

DANNI. Mabel, how much *blood* did Romulus *take*?!

ROMULUS. (*steps into room, and slightly to his right, before* L. *night table, to keep sightlines clear for CAMERON's upcoming entrance*) No *take* blood! (*points at MABEL*) This happen, so I stop!

MABEL. Isn't it *terrible*?!

HILARY. (*forgetting caution anymore, as is BUGSY,*

too, as they come to their feet) Mabel, are you nuts? You look absolutely *fantastic*!

MABEL. (*now we find out why she's sobbing:*) Of course I do! But how am I going to afford *all new uniforms*?!

(*Then CAMERON Enters from bathroom and stops: the pajama-jacket comes to his knees, the cuffs of the pajama-pants are rolled up almost that high, too; he looks like a man being swallowed by a multi-colored tent.*)

CAMERON. *Mabel*! You look marvelous! This is ghastly!

DANNI. (*realizes*) My *drinking*-glass! *That's* how this happened! Oh, I *knew* I shouldn't have shared!

CAMERON. Everybody stand right where they are! Don't move! If Mabel can get this thin after eating an entire pound of fudge, just because of contact with Danni, we'll have to *quarantine* this room!

DANNI. You mean—anyone who comes in contact with me will *have* to eat *fudge* and *lose weight*?!

CAMERON. *Exactly*! So if you value your *metabolisms, everybody—don't* go near *Danni*!

(*There is stasis for the count of three, with ALL frozen in place where they are; then, in a simultaneous movement, MABEL springs forward to embrace and go cheek-to-cheek with DANNI on one side, while HILARY does the same on the other side, and BUGSY* [*who's not anywhere near as thin as he'd like to be*] *dives to his knees and embraces her legs, his cheek pillowed against her thigh; all three huggers wear beatific smiles of joy, while DANNI smiles helplessly, and ROMULUS just stares blankly, and a super-chagrined CAMERON smacks his forehead with one palm and shuts his eyes in hoepless despair, as—)*

THE CURTAIN FALLS
—End of Act One—

ACT TWO

Curtain rises on DANNI's room, about 7 A.M. the following morning. Drapes are open, but French doors are closed. DANNI's suitcase, CAMERON's topcoat and medical bag, and stack of candy boxes have all been cleared. The room and the garden outside are bright and sunny.

At curtain-rise, we find DANNI and MABEL seated on chest, and BUGSY seated in desk chair, on the telephone. DANNI is in an attractive nightgown, MABEL is in the top half of ROMULUS's pajamas, and BUGSY is in the bottom half of ROMULUS's pajamas and an undershirt—and *his sunglasses. DANNI and MABEL stare out front, kind of glassy-eyed, but BUGSY is jolly and enthusiastic as he completes his conversation:*

BUGSY. Right! . . . Perfect! . . . She'll *be* there! . . . *Ciao*, Baby! (*hangs up, turns in chair to face duo on chest*) That makes *five*! This thing is a gold mine! (*chortles happily, turns back to phone, lifts it, starts to dial*)

DANNI. Bugsy, much as I appreciate all your efforts on my behalf—

BUGSY. (*busily dialing*) *My* behalf, *too,* sweetheart! A manager gets fifteen percent! (*listens a second on phone, hangs up*) Line's busy.

DANNI. (*stands*) Bugsy, will you *stop*? I don't know if I *want* to go around infecting chocolate factories! It just doesn't seem—*sanitary*!

BUGSY. Relax! If the chocolate people don't mind, why should you?

DANNI. But they *do* mind! None of them will hire me over-the-counter!

MABEL. That's only because of the Board of Health, dear. They'd go out of business if the board found out they were selling tainted candy.

DANNI. I wish you wouldn't use that term. You make me feel like a leper!

BUGSY. Listen, Danni, I've got them all *competing* with one another for your services! It goes *up* ten thousand bucks each new company!

DANNI. Honestly, Bugsy, when you *first* brought this up, yesterday, it didn't seem *so* bad. I mean, standing beside the conveyor-belt just kind of *touching* the candy as it went by—but *this* plan of yours—!

BUGSY. (*stands, goes over to her*) It wasn't *my* plan, doll! The candy-makers thought it up.

DANNI. But it feels so—*sneaky*!

MABEL. It *is* sneaky—but in such a good cause! And it's the only way to taint the candy without the Board of Health catching on.

DANNI. I can't. Even for fifty-thousand a throw, I just *can't*!

MABEL. Oh, of *course* you can! It'll be just like your *old* job—bikini and all!

BUGSY. *All* high-paying jobs should be so easy! They close the factory up for the night, leave the gate unlatched at the rear, you tiptoe in, go to the chocolate vat, strip down to your swimsuit, and—

DANNI. I know, I know! But I'm not even sure if I can *swim* in melted chocolate! Can *anybody*?

BUGSY. Just keep one hand on the rim of the tank.

DANNI. I need *both* hands to *swim,* if I'm going to work up a *sweat*!

MABEL. Maybe not, dear. I understand the chocolate's *very* warm.

BUGSY. Come on, Danni, cheer up. At fifty-thousand a dip, you should be walking on air!

DANNI. But I'll be swimming in chocolate!

MABEL. But then you'll be rolling in dough!

BUGSY. This swimming-bit is your own fault, remember! You *nixed* their *original* idea!

DANNI. Bugsy, for all the money in the *world*, I was *not* going to *spit* into those vats! (*THUD-THUD-THUD*)

TRIO. Come *in*, Romulus!

ROMULUS. (*Enters bearing stack of candy boxes*) Fudge. (*sets boxes on desk*) Enjoy. (*Exits*)

MABEL. I can't *look* at another piece of fudge!

BUGSY. Me, neither! At least *you've* got something to *show* for it.

DANNI. Why *aren't* you any thinner, Bugsy?

BUGSY. Who knows? Maybe male metabolism is different from women's.

MABEL. (*rubs* [*unseen*] *hollow of one arm*) I *hope* Doctor Barkley's finished checking our blood! I never want to *look* at another needle as long as I live!

BUGSY. Five'll get you ten I didn't catch a damned thing!

DANNI. (*annoyed at the memory*) You sure *tried* hard enough!

BUGSY. Aw, what's a little kiss between friends!

DANNI. You didn't tell me you *slobber*!

MABEL. You *let* him kiss you?

DANNI. Hell, no! He *slobbers*!

MABEL. Then it's just as well you didn't kiss him. *You'd* have been sharing *his* spit! (*a KNOCK at hall door*)

TRIO. Come *in* . . . !

CAMERON. (*Enters, dressed in shirt, tie, etc., but also in a lab smock*) Why aren't you eating your fudge?!

MABEL. I'm not taking another bite till you get the blood-test results!

CAMERON. I was talking to *Danni*!

MABEL. (*eyes wide with hope, stands up*) You mean —*I* don't have to?

CAMERON. I guess not. All the blood-tests are completed, and you're off the hook, Mabel.

BUGSY. You mean she *hasn't* got Danni's disease? Then how come she's so *skinny* all at once?

CAMERON. Far as I can determine—Mabel *had* the disease—long enough to drop all that weight—and then she got *over* it! Some people *do* that—catch a germ, or get bitten by a spider, and they have an *initial* reaction—then throw the infestation off.

MABEL. (*starts for hall door*) Then if you'll excuse me, I have a date with some mouthwash—then a T-bone steak!

DANNI. But Mabel—what if you're *contagious*?

MABEL. No problem. I've always *wanted* to go swimming in chocolate!

CAMERON. You are *not* contagious, Mabel. Not a *trace* of Danni's chemistry left in you.

MABEL. Damn. I could've *used* that fifty-thousand!

CAMERON. What fifty-thousand? What's she talking about? Swimming in *what* chocolate?

BUGSY. (*quickly*) She had this nightmare last night—candy manufacturers were paying her a fortune to infect their vats!

CAMERON. What a hideous thought! I'm glad *Danni* doesn't harbor such insane ambitions!

DANNI. (*forging a smile*) That's very—*trusting* of you, Doctor.

CAMERON. Anyhow, you may as well hear *all* the results. Strange the way everybody's metabolism differs. Out of four people—four different results.

BUGSY. So *tell* us!

CAMERON. Okay, it's this way—for Danni—no change.

BUGSY. *Great*—! (*get's a curious look from CAMERON, immediately adds:*) —*Godfrey*, what a shame!

CAMERON. Don't worry. If there's a cure—I'll find it!

BUGSY. (*we sense his glee, even if CAMERON doesn't*) Even if it takes years—and *years*—and *YEARS*—!

DANNI. And Bugsy—?

CAMERON. (*shakes his head*) Not a *drop* of contamination. His blood is perfectly normal in all respects.

BUGSY. Don't fret, Doc. *I* can't swim, *anyhow*!

CAMERON. Huh—? Oh—you meant—that chocolate-vat thing—! (*smiles slightly*) For a moment, I didn't realize you were joking.

BUGSY. (*wistfully*) For a moment, neither did I!

DANNI. But what about *Hilary*?

BUGSY. Yeah, what's the score on *her*, Doc?

CAMERON. Again, another case of a different metabolism producing different results. See, Danni remained contaminated, Mister McCorkle remained normal, Mabel Chubbs caught the infestation but threw it off in a short time—but Hilary—!

DUO. *Yes . . .* ?

CAMERON. (*just as bathroom door starts to open*) I'm afraid *Hilary's* chemistry conquered the contamination by *reversing* its effect—! (*door is fully open now, and we see HILARY—in robe and slippers—looking* [*via cotton rolls and padding*] *about forty pounds plumper than she was*)

HILARY. (*stands in doorway, then remarks sardonically:*) *Tell* me about it!

BUGSY. Now-now, sweetheart, it's gonna be okay. I mean, this *is* a Fat Farm, and you've got till next *Monday* to get rid of the poundage—!

DANNI. What's next Monday?

BUGSY. The new Paramount deal—she has to go in for *costume*-fittings

HILARY. If I can fit through the *gate*!

BUGSY. You'll be fine, baby, fine! Just hang in there with the carrot-sticks and lettuce—

CAMERON. I'm afraid that won't do her much good, Mister McCorkle. In her present condition, even a piece of *celery* will increase her weight.

HILARY. (*horrified*) *WHAT*?!

DANNI. Oh, this is dreadful! Doctor, can't you *do* something?

CAMERON. I'm not sure—at the rate she's expanding, even *lipo-suction* wouldn't help!

DANNI. Wait! I have an idea! What if Hilary went to the Amazon, to the very place where I ran into that swarm of cocoa wasps—I'm *sure* they'd still *be* there—and if *she* could manage to get stung—!

CAMERON. It'd never work—not with her body-chemistry producing an *opposite* effect! She'd *still* be fat—

HILARY. And covered with *lumps*—

BUGSY. And she'd *never* outrun that alligator!

DANNI. But Cameron—it's worth a *try*, isn't it?

BUGSY. (*dubiously*) I dunno—I read someplace that travel is *broadening*.

HILARY. Not as fast as *I* am! . . . Still, if there's even a *chance*—

BUGSY. (*hopefully*) What do you say, Doc?

CAMERON. (*who has been staring rapturously at DANNI since her last line*) You—you called me "Cameron"!

DANNI. Well, if you're going to continue to *room* with me, "Doctor Barkley" sounds *silly*!

CAMERON. (*steps toward her*) Danni!

DANNI. (*steps toward him*) Cameron!

BUGSY. (*steps between them just as they start to lunge for one another*) *Hold* it! What about *Hilary*?

CAMERON. I don't know. I honestly don't know. Of course, if I came up with a cure for *Danni,* there's just the outside chance that it'd work for Hilary, *too*—I mean, despite her *opposite* chemistry, whatever restored Danni to *normalcy* might do the same for *her*!

HILARY. Then why are you just *standing* there! Get to *work* on it!

CAMERON. (*to DANNI*) She's right. I mustn't procrastinte any longer, darling!

DANNI. You—you called me "darling"! Oh, Cameron!

CAMERON. Oh, Danni!

BUGSY. (*who'd stepped back, once more jumps between them in mid-lunge*) The *cure*, damn it, the *cure*!

HILARY. And *hurry*!

CAMERON. (*with professionalism restored*) Right! (*starts for hall door*) I'll start working on it immediately. And then—when I return—!

DANNI. —to my waiting arms—!

HILARY/BUGSY. (*as CAMERON half-turns toward DANNI*) The *cure*!

CAMERON. (*guiltily*) Right! (*Exits to hall; an instant later, BELL RINGS for a few seconds*)

HILARY. *Finally*! Now I can get *out* of this place! (*opens French doors*)

BUGSY. You're leaving the *clinic*? What about the *cure*?

HILARY. I'm *only* going to my *room,* Bugsy. How *could* I leave? I have nothing to *wear*!

DANNI. But Hilary, are you sure you're not contagious?

HILARY. Right now, I don't *give* a damn!

BUGSY. Don't worry, sweetheart, everything's going to be fine, just fine!

HILARY. And if he *doesn't* find a cure?

BUGSY. You can *still* have a career! Overweight isn't necessarily a problem: Look at Liz Taylor, Judy Garland, Shelley Winters, Lainie Kazan—! There are still *plenty* of *fat parts* for a talented actress—I mean, *big* parts—!

HILARY. (*sarcastically*) Sure there are! *If* somebody decides to film the life-story of the *Goodyear blimp! (Exits R. into garden)*

DANNI. I feel just terrible about all this! It's *my* fault—coming here, infecting all these nice people—!

BUGSY. Look on the bright side—soon as you're out of here, you'll be *swimming* in money!

DANNI. You mean in *chocolate*!

BUGSY. That reminds me—I'm waiting for callbacks from all those companies about your contract with them—(*starts out through French doors in quiet pursuit of HILARY*) If I'm not back, take any messages, will you? I gave them your room-number.

DANNI. But Bugsy—under the circumstances—I don't think my *conscience* will let me go *through* with it!

BUGSY. (*horrified, steps back into room*) *What* circumstances?!

DANNI. That *body*-chemistry thing! Any chocolate *I've* been swimming in might just as well make people *fat!* If it could happen to *Hilary*—

BUGSY. A fluke! A one-in-a-million mischance! Don't even *think* about it!

DANNI. You're just *saying* that because of the *money* you'd lose!

BUGSY. (*draws himself up in offended dignity*) *Danni! What* do you think I *am*?!

DANNI. (*arms akimbo*) A Hollywood manager!

BUGSY. You watch your language! (*Exits through French doors and off* R.)

DANNI. (*calls after him*) If the shoe fits—! (*stops as MABEL bursts into room from hall*)

MABEL. How *could* you let me go *out* there like *this*?!

DANNI. You *forgot* you were wearing that pajama-top?

MABEL. (*has already closed door and is crossing past DANNI toward closet*) Until *Romulus* spotted me!

DANNI. Why would *he* be upset? I mean, he *lent* Cameron those pajamas?!

MABEL. (*has closet door open, now*) He likes the way I *look* in them! I've got to get dressed!

DANNI. But why in such a dreadful *hurry*?

MABEL. Romulus says he's head-over-heels in *love* with me!

DANNI. Romulus said *that*?!

MABEL. Not in so many words—Romulus doesn't *know* so many words—but that *look* in his eye told me all I wanted to know! Excuse me! (*Exits into closet, shuts door*)

DANNI. But—?! (*THUD-THUD-THUD*) Oh, dear!

ROMULUS. (*opens hall door, peeks around the edge of it at DANNI*) Peek-a-boo!

DANNI. Romulus, don't come in! I've got to get dressed!

ROMULUS. Where Mabel?

DANNI. Uh—how should *I* know?

ROMULUS. (*crossing room*) Not worry. I find! (*Exits to garden, crooning in his booming bass voice:*) *Ma*-bellll—!

DANNI. (*rushes to closet door, leans close to it to remark:*) I think you were *right*! He's like a lovesick *puppy*—well, a *Saint Bernard* puppy!

MABEL. (*off*) I'm *dressing* as fast as I *can*!

DANNI. That reminds me—*I'd* better get some clothes on, myself! Hand me a dress, will you?

MABEL. (*off*) Which one—?

DANNI. Just grab. You can't see in the dark, anyhow!

MABEL. (*pops out, hands dress to DANNI*) What about shoes and underwear?

DANNI. (*starting* L.) My suitcase is in the bathroom. There's no *room* in the closet with all the *traffic* goes through there!

(*She will Exit into bathroom and MABEL back into closet; the moment both doors have closed, there is a KNOCK at hall door; after a moment, door opens and AUGUSTA* [*now in a different dress from before*] *Enters.*)

AUGUSTA. Danni—? Miss Dawn—?

DANNI. (*off*) In here! I'm dressing!

AUGUSTA. (*goes nearer bathroom door*) I have some telephone-messages for you—some very *strange* telephone messages!

DANNI. (*off; knows what they are; there is a pause before she replies cautiously:*) Uh—*thank* you, Miss Fairfax! Could you just—leave them on the desk?

AUGUSTA. (*takes folded paper from pocket, glances at it, hesitates, then:*) Actually—I wanted to *discuss* them with you . . .

DANNI. (*off; pause; then:*) Oh . . . all right. Soon as I come out, okay?

AUGUSTA. Yes, dear. Thank you. (*will move to chest, and sit, unfolding paper and scanning it, mumbling:*) I simply can't *understand* this—

DANNI. (*off*) *What* did you say—?

AUGUSTA. Nothing, dear. Just muttering to myself. Get dressed, and then we'll talk.

DANNI. (*off*) Uh-sure. I'll only be a minute. (*then ROMULUS lumbers in from garden, sees AUGUSTA, stops*)

AUGUSTA. Romulus! You simply *mustn't* come into a guest's room without *knocking* on the *door*!

ROMULUS. (*points at French doors*) *Glass* might break.

AUGUSTA. (*reluctantly*) You have a point. What is it you want?

ROMULUS. (*hungrily*) Mabel!

AUGUSTA. (*uneasy*) Nurse Chubbs? What do you want her—*for* . . . ?

ROMULUS. (*droolingly*) Love!

AUGUSTA. (*comes to her feet*) Why, Romulus! You *know* the clinic by-laws militate against fraternization among the staff members!

ROMULUS. (*leans over her*) *Bad* by-laws!

AUGUSTA. (*takes a tiny backstep*) Yes, they *are*, aren't they!

ROMULUS. You change!

AUGUSTA. (*nods several times, taking two more backsteps*) At the very next board meeting!

ROMULUS. You promise?

AUGUSTA. (*her mind going slightly*) Me promise!

ROMULUS. (*all smiles*) Good! (*will Exit to hall, happily caroling:*) *Ma*-bell! . . . *Yoo*-hoo! . . . *Maaaaa*-bellll—! (*door closes, and he is gone*)

AUGUSTA. (*sags down onto chest, slightly shaken*) Life used to be so *easy* around here—! (*abruptly stands again*) I'd better find Mabel and *warn* her! (*will start toward garden*) Maybe she can take her vacation *early . . .* or change her *name . . .* or wear a *disguise*—!

(*Exits* R. *into garden; a moment later, MABEL, now wearing [becomingly] one of DANNI's dresses—but with low-heeled white nurse-shoes on her feet—creeps cautiously out of closet, looks around, then tiptoes toward hall; just before she gets to door, bathroom door opens and DANNI—now fully dressed—comes out.*)

DANNI. All set! (*reacts*) Oh! Where did Miss Fairfax go? (*looks closely*) Isn't that one of *my* dresses, Mabel?

MABEL. I hope you don't mind! My uniform fits me like an oversized *toga*!

DANNI. Not at all, Mabel. That's really quite *becoming* on you! I'm almost *jealous*! But those *shoes* don't do a *thing* for the outfit!

MABEL. I know. But I can *run* faster in these! If *Romulus* spots me—!

DANNI. He's really got you *spooked*, hasn't he!

MABEL. Don't get me wrong—I *like* Romulus! It's just that—in his present state of mind—he might suddenly *grab* me into his arms, and—Have you *seen* those arms?! He can hug a side of beef into *hamburger*! I might survive if I were still at my *fighting*-weight—fat makes a nice cushion—but built the way I am today—!

DANNI. (*nods*) He'd pop you like a pretzel!

MABEL. To put it *mildly*! (*then a brief wistful smile illuminates her face, on:*) But *what* a way to *go*! (*then, with sudden return to decorum, adds in serene tones:*) Well, if you'll excuse me, I've got to run for my life. Have a nice day. (*Exits into hall, shutting door behind her*)

ROMULUS. (*off* L.) *Maaa*-bellll—!
MABEL. (*off* L.) *Yaaaaaah!*

(*As DANNI winces in sympathy, we hear THUNDEROUS FOOTFALLS galloping outside hall door, in sync with MABEL's scream, which continues awhile until it, and the footfalls, fade with distance.*)

DANNI. (*thoughtfully*) Maybe she can lose herself among the after-breakfast joggers . . . !

BUGSY. (*enters from garden, almost dancing*) Where the heck are my clothes? I can't drive back to L.A. like *this*! Did I leave them in the *closet*?

DANNI. (*resignedly shrugs*) Where *else*?

BUGSY. Ah, good! (*opens closet door, starts to enter, turns to her for:*) No *peek*-ing . . . ! (*goes in, shuts door*)

DANNI. (*disgustedly*) Don't flatter yourself! (*then remembers, goes near closet door*) Bugsy, I forgot—I think some of those candy people have started *calling* you!

BUGSY. (*off*) Aren't you *sure*?

DANNI. Miss Fairfax stopped by a few minutes ago—said I had some *unusual* messages. Ten-to-one they were for *you*!

BUGSY. (*off*) *Great*! Where are they?

DANNI. I guess she's still got them *with* her! What are those candy people *calling* about, anyhow?

BUGSY. (*off*) Well, they had to clear the deal with their boards of directors, of course, before we get the go-ahead. But don't sweat, baby, you're a *shoo*-in for the job!

DANNI. You mean a *dive*-in, don't you?!

BUGSY. (*off*) That's what I love in a woman—a sense of humor!

DANNI. By the way—how in the world did you *reach*

all those people so *early*? You didn't have their *home* phone-numbers, did you?

BUGSY. (*off*) They're not *in* L.A.! Most'f 'em are back east — Chicago, St. Louis, like that. Their offices have been open for *hours*! . . . Damn, where's my other shoe — ?

DANNI. It's *got* to be in there *someplace*!

BUGSY. (*off*) Ah! Got it!

DANNI. Bugsy — I'm starting to have second thoughts about this candy-company deal. What's going to *happen* to me if too many chocolate-lovers turn out like *Hilary*?!

BUGSY. (*emerges from closet, dressed as we first saw him, carrying bottom half of ROMULUS's pajamas*) Not to worry. By *then* you and I will be sharing more than a million under-the-counter *bucks*!

DANNI. But they might *sue* me — try to get the money *back* — !

BUGSY. No way! To sue you, they'd have to admit why they *hired* you!

DANNI. The *customers* might sue me!

BUGSY. The customers won't *know* about you! Besides, can you imagine their *testimony* if they *did*? (*in a weepy voice:*) "*I* ate ten pounds of *fudge* and gained *weight*!" (*normal voice*) The judge would laugh them out of court! You're in the *clear*, kid!

DANNI. Maybe *I* am, but my conscience *isn't*! I couldn't *do* that to those poor people!

BUGSY. *Poor* people can't *afford* ten pounds of fudge!

(*Then BOTH react as ROMULUS gallops in from garden, sights on pajama-bottoms, grabs them from BUGSY's hands, shakes them hopefully, then slumps unhappily — then unhappiness turns to dan-*

gerous suspicion, and he steps forward to tower over a cowering DUO on:)

ROMULUS. Where *Mabel*?!

DANNI. The *top* half, Romulus, she was wearing the *top* half!

ROMULUS. (*looks at pajama-bottoms, shakes them once more, relaxes*) Oh, yeah. (*tosses bottoms back to BUGSY, starts for hall door*) I go find! *Ma*-bel—! (*stops as door opens and CAMERON hurries in*)

CAMERON. Romulus! Just the man I'm looking for! Quick, go to the kitchen, get a pitcher and a bunch of glasses, and bring them to the lab!

ROMULUS. (*wistfully*) *Now*?

CAMERON. Of *course* now! Hurry, man, hurry! I'll *meet* you there in two minutes!

(*ROMULUS sighs, but obediently trots out into garden, and CAMERON turns and starts back toward hall door, but stops and turns, at:*)

DANNI. Cameron! Did you *do* it?!

CAMERON. I think so . . . I hope so . . . It's a long shot, but—things can't get much *worse*!

DANNI. Oh, darling, that's marvelous! I just *know* it's going to work!

BUGSY. (*aghast*) But it *can't*! It *mustn't*! Not *now*, when we're on the brink of—

CAMERON. McCorkle, what's your problem? On *what* brink?

DANNI. (*quickly*) He just signed Hilary to star in *The Kate Smith Story*! Now they'll have to call the picture off!

CAMERON. Don't worry, McCorkle—she can always handle the part with makeup! . . . *Lots* of makeup! (*Exits to hall, leaving door open*)

DANNI. Hilary! I've got to go tell her the good news! (*will dash* U.R. *and Exit, during:*) Which way to her room?

BUGSY. (*deflated and glum*) Just follow the sound of brokenhearted *sobbing*! (*then turns as AUGUSTA rushes in from hall, paper in hand*)

AUGUSTA. Danni? Where are you? We never *did* discuss these *messages*!

BUGSY. (*takes paper from her hand*) Here, *I'll* take those!

AUGUSTA. But—

BUGSY. It's kosher—I'm her personal manager! (*starts to read messages eagerly, reacts with dismay, then reads them out loud:*) "Crackpot"?! . . . "Lunatic"?! . . . "The deal's *off*, Nutso"?! . . . "*Forget* it, Screwball"?! (*crumples paper, turns furiously to AUGUSTA*) What's the *meaning* of this?!

AUGUSTA. (*startled*) I have no idea! That's what *I* wanted to ask *Danni*!

BUGSY. You must have *some* idea, woman! When did they call? What did you *say* to them?

AUGUSTA. *I* never spoke with *any* of the callers. They were all handled by Florence, the usual way.

BUGSY. Who's Florence?!

AUGUSTA. Our switchboard operator, of course. She takes *all* incoming messages!

BUGSY. (*the dawn of horror*) Wait a minute—switchboard—the *usual* way—what did Florence *say* to these people?!

AUGUSTA. Why—just the regulation greeting—"Good morning. Fairfax Clinic for Digestive Psychoses . . ."?

BUGSY. *Digestive Psychoses*?! No *wonder* they thought I was a nutcake! (*looms over her*) Why couldn't

Florence say "*Fat Farm*"? They think I'm in a *mental asylum*!

AUGUSTA. But "Fat Farm" is such an *unpleasant* term—!

BUGSY. (*an incoherent scream*) *Aaaargh*! (*starts for garden*) I need air! *Lots* of air!

(*Even as he Exits, ROMULUS enters through still-open hall door, carrying a large tray on which reposes a central pitcher surrounded by half a dozen empty water-glasses; the liquid in the pitcher is creamy brown, about the color of dairy-made chocolate milk* [*which you should* use *for it*].)

AUGUSTA. (*reacts*) Not *more* chocolate?! My guests will be coming here in a *mob*! Where did that *come* from?

ROMULUS. (*will set tray on coffeetable, during:*) Doctor Fairbanks make.

AUGUSTA. Why? Wasn't the fudge *enough*?

ROMULUS. (*shrugs*) He said bring it.

AUGUSTA. (*goes to tray, stares down at it*) But what *is* this stuff? I mean, we don't *keep* cocoa-mix on the premises—? (*will curiously fill one glass from pitcher*)

ROMULUS. What doing?

AUGUSTA. As head of this institute, I should *know* what's going on in it! (*takes healthy swallow—about half a glassful—and reacts like a person who just bit into a lemon*) Aghhh! This tastes positively *terrible*!

ROMULUS. (*takes glass from her hand, curiously, sips*) Yummy! (*drains rest of glass*)

AUGUSTA. (*suddenly sways, back of hand to forehead*) I feel—so *strange,* all at once . . . !

ROMULUS. (*replacing emptied glass on tray*) *Romulus* feel *fine*!

AUGUSTA. The room—it's spinning—faster and faster—(*staggers to bed*) I've got to lie down—! (*flops on her back on bed*) I think—I think I'm starting to pass out! (*abruptly goes unconscious*)

ROMULUS. (*smiles, goes to bed, flips coverlet to conceal her from head to foot, on:*) Nighty-night! (*moves toward hall door, now, at a happy jog*) Mabel! . . . *Maaaa*-belll—! (*he is gone; a moment later, an eager HILARY, still plump, rushes in from garden, DANNI and a gloomy BUGSY following her into room*)

HILARY. Oh! Is *this* it? In this pitcher?

DANNI. I *hope* so! I mean—it's surrounded by *glasses*!

BUGSY. So what? Why so *cheerful*?

DANNI. It means we don't have to take it in a *hypo*!

HILARY. (*reaches for glass*) I don't care *how* we take it, as long as it *fixes* things!

DANNI. Wait! We don't *know* this is Cameron's cure!

HILARY. (*straightens, leaving glass on tray*) You're right! But—where *is* your doctor, anyhow?!

CAMERON. (*just Entering from hall*) Right here! Had to clean up the mess on the lab-table. (*points to tray*) Well, folks—there it is!

DANNI. Will it work?

CAMERON. Can't be *certain*, of course—but chemically, far as I can determine, it's *precisely* what's needed to neutralize the chocolate problem.

HILARY. (*now pouring a glassful*) Thank heaven!

CAMERON. Careful! You'd better not have *too much* of the stuff! Not till I see the results.

HILARY. (*now holding full glass*) How much *is* too much? (*DANNI, meantime, will be pouring glassful of her own, now*)

CAMERON. Well, how much did you have in that *other* glass?

BUGSY. *Nobody* had that other glass.

CAMERON. (*picks glass up, stares at its inner coating*) *Somebody* must have—just *look* at the *dregs* here . . .

HILARY. *I* sure didn't.

DANNI. Me, neither!

CAMERON. (*sets glass back on tray*) Then *who—*? . . . Unless *Mabel—*?

BUGSY. With her new figure, I don't think Mabel would *want* to be cured!

CAMERON. *That's* true enough—but then, who *had* some of this stuff? In the wrong alimentary canal, it could be *dangerous*!

DANNI. Why? What's *in* it?

CAMERON. Well, I had to counteract the chemistry of the *chocolate*, so I used every *opposite* thing I could think of—most of the ingredients would be meaningless names to you, but for the most part, it's a compound of milk and turkey-gravy.

TRIO. *Yucchhh*!

CAMERON. That was to offset the chocolate's *caffeine*, see?

BUGSY. Milk and gravy?!

CAMERON. Milk and turkey are packed with L-tryptophane, a natural sedative! That's why people get drowsy after taking hot milk at bedtime—or fall asleep on the sofa after Thanksgiving dinner.

DANNI. So *that* counteracts the *caffeine* from the chocolate—! Of course! What *else* is in this stuff?

HILARY. *Wait*! I don't want to *know*. Milk-and-gravy is about *all* I can handle without upchucking!

CAMERON. It's too complicated to describe, anyhow.

DANNI. So now what—?

CAMERON. (*shrugs*) Bottoms up!

HILARY/DANNI. (*They look at one another, then gamely raise their glasses in a sort of toast to one another, on:*) Cheers! (*they drink—making awful faces—until the glasses are drained; then:*) *Aaaackkk*! (*they set the glasses on the tray*)

DANNI. (*still making faces, contorting her mouth against the taste*) Cameron . . . if you ever come over to my apartment—stay *out* of my kitchen!

BUGSY. Hilary? Sweetheart, how do *you* feel?

HILARY. (*a tentative hand to her stomach*) I'm not sure . . . but I've felt much *better* than this, that's for sure!

BUGSY. You think you might upchuck?

HILARY. Please! Don't even *say* the word, the way *I* feel at the moment—!

CAMERON. But you *mustn't* upchuck! You've got to let the medication start *working*!

HILARY. (*lurches toward garden*) Then I need fresh air—*oceans* of it—!

BUGSY. (*hurrying out with her*) Easy, baby, easy! Think of your old figure—think of the Goodyear blimp—! (*they are gone*)

DANNI. (*face less contorted now*) Well? When do I find out if I'm cured?

CAMERON. I'm afraid it'll mean another blood-test . . .

DANNI. Cameron—were there any *vampires* on your family tree—?!

CAMERON. (*pleasantly*) Probably.

DANNI. (*gives him a look, then smiles and goes into his arms*) Remind me to eat plenty of *garlic* on our first date!

CAMERON. We can always go to an *Italian* restaurant . . .

(*Then BOTH look hallward as MABEL Enters, her eyes bright and shining.*)

MABEL. (*rapturously*) I'm *engaged*!

CAMERON. To *who*?

DANNI. Mabel! You don't mean—you and *Romulus*—?!

MABEL. (*ecstatically*) You better believe it!

DANNI. But—what about his *arms*—turning beef into hamburger—popping you like a pretzel?!

MABEL. *That* was the *old* Romulus!

CAMERON. What do you mean.

MABEL. (*looks back toward hallway*) Come on *in*, honeycakes!

DANNI/CAMERON. (*face-to-face for an incredulous:*) "Honeycakes"?!

(*Then they gape and step apart as ROMULUS Enters from hall, almost shyly: He is now normal height and breadth, and the "neanderthal look" is totally gone* [*okay, so he was padded and shoe-lifted from the start of this play till now; wanted to save you* some *surprises*].)

ROMULUS. (*in nice, intelligent voice*) Hi there, folks.

MABEL. (*embracing him*) Isn't he absolutely *gorgeous*?!

ROMULUS. Nowhere near as gorgeous as *you*, my dearest darling!

CAMERON. Romulus, this is *miraculous*! You even *sound* like a normal person! But how did this happen? What in the world could have—have—(*a sudden thought; he whirls to look toward tray, points excitedly*) *You* drank from that other glass!

DANNI. (*embraces him*) Oh, darling! You're a medical genius! You not only can control body-size—you can cure *stupidity*!

ROMULUS. *My* theory is, it was my *height* interfering with my brain-power. The blood just couldn't *pump* that high!

(*Then HILARY and BUGSY rush in from garden, hand-in-hand; she's still in robe, but her face and figure are back to their original size.*)

HILARY. Look! Look! I'm cured!

BUGSY. Doc, you've got to *bottle* that stuff! We can make a *zillion* from fat ladies all over the globe!

CAMERON. *Damn*! I hope I can *remember* everything I put into it! And the *proportions* are important, too! I must know *exactly* how much everybody drank, the precise state of their endocrine system at the moment, the—

BUGSY/HILARY. (*just spotting DUO near door*) *ROMULUS*!

BUGSY. What *happened* to him?!

HILARY. He looks absolutely *marvelous*!

ROMULUS. And I *talk* a lot better, too!

BUGSY. Did I say a *zillion*?! We'll make a *billion*-zillion! It makes fat ladies thin, it makes a Goliath into a Cary Grant—!

MABEL. —and it *definitely* improves his *conversation*—

ROMULUS. (*a cooing lover*) Aw, my itsy-bitsy cootchy-wootchy huggy-bunny sweetcakes!

MABEL. (*amends, with less enthusiasm*) —*sort* of.

CAMERON. I've *got* to get this all *down* before I forget it! Let me think—Danni had one glassful, Hilary had one glassful, Romulus had one glassful—

ROMULUS. *Half* a glassful, actually.

DANNI. Why did you stop at only *half* a glassful?

ROMULUS. Because Miss Fairfax drank the *first* half . . . (*then he realizes, as do others, and joins them in:*)

ALL. *Miss Fairfax*?!

CAMERON. When?

MABEL. Where?

DANNI. Why?

ROMULUS. A few minutes ago, right here, to see what Doctor Barkley was giving her guests.

CAMERON. Damn! We may not be out of the woods, *yet*! Who *knows* what effect that could have upon a woman of upper middle age?! Women that old have digestive problems, hormone problems, mineral-retention problems—!

DANNI. We've got to *find* her!

ROMULUS. But I *know* where she is!

OTHERS. *Where*?!

ROMULUS. (*points*) Right *there*!

(*ALL immediately rush* U.S. *and flank bed, HILARY/ BUGSY/DANNI on* R. *side, MABEL/ROMULUS/ CAMERON on* L. *side*)

BUGSY. She's so *still* . . . !

HILARY. Is she *asleep* . . . ?

MABEL. In a *coma* . . . ?

DANNI. *Dead* . . . ?!

ROMULUS. Why don't we *ask* her?

CAMERON. Ask her *what*?

ROMULUS. Well, *Danni* could start.

DANNI. By saying what?

ROMULUS. (*gives a What-else*? shrug, on:) "*Who's* been sleeping in *my* bed?"!

MABEL. (*elbows him*) Rommy, that's not funny!

ROMULUS. I never *had* a sense of humor before. Thought I'd give it a try.

DANNI. We've *got* to know how that stuff *affected* her! (*prods form on bed*) Wake *up*, Miss Fairfax—!

HILARY. *Please*, Gussie—!

CAMERON. Come *on*, Gus—!

AUGUSTA. (*we hear her yawn, then see her arms as she stretches, then says:*) How many times do I have to *tell* you people I *hate* that nickname! (*will start sitting up, on:*) Makes me sound like a *man*—!

(*On final word, coverlet falls away from her face and upper torso, and we see that she has a full bushy beard and mustache; others stand open-mouthed and speechless with shock for a moment; then:*)

BUGSY. (*his brain going once again into high gear:*) Miss Fairfax, do you have any *idea* how much money a *woman* can make on TV endorsing *razor-blades* . . . ?! (*and as he rubs his hands together in glee, and AUGUSTA stares at him in blank puzzlement, and OTHERS all shut their eyes and kind of* shrink *in chagrin and despair*—)

THE CURTAIN FALLS

—End of Play—

Stage Setting
for
"OH, FUDGE!"

1) Settee and coffeetable
2) Closet
3) Garden backdrop, French doors
4) Draw-drapes and pull-cord
5) Bed, night-tables with lamps
6) Mattress-high chest-of-drawers
7) Bathroom
8) Tall potted plant
9) Clinic corridor
10) Lightswitch, writing-desk, chair, phone